Camping

BY ALLAN MOREY

AMICUS HIGH INTEREST • AMICUS INK

Amicus High Interest and Amicus Ink are imprints of Amicus
P.O. Box 1329, Mankato, MN 56002
www.amicuspublishing.us

Library of Congress Cataloging-in-Publication Data
Morey, Allan.
Camping / by Allan Morey.
     pages cm. – (Great Outdoors)
Includes webography.
Includes index.
Summary: "This photo-illustrated book for elementary students
describes where to camp and ways to have fun. Includes
information on tents, RVs or motorhomes, avoiding wild animals,
and campfire safety"– Provided by publisher.
ISBN 978-1-60753-796-0 (library binding)
ISBN 978-1-68151-016-3 (ebook)
ISBN 978-1-68152-075-9 (paperback)
1. Camping–Juvenile literature. I. Title.
GV191.7.M67 2017
796.54–dc23

                              2015023215

Editor: Wendy Dieker
Series Designer: Kathleen Petelinsek
Book Designer: Tracy Myers
Photo Researcher: Derek Brown

Photo Credits: People images/iStock cover, Randy Faris /
Corbis 5, Jay Si / iStock 6, Jens Ottoson / Shutterstock 9,
Vereshchagin Dmitry / Shutterstock 10, Paige Falk / iStock 13,
Monkey Business Images / Shutterstock 14, Sasha Burkard
/ Shutterstock 17, Mat Hayward / Shutterstock 19, Susan E.
Degginger / Alamy 20, pretty foto / Alamy 22-23, Jamie Grill
Photography / Tetra Images / Corbis 25, Steve Hix / Somos
Images / Corbis 26, oliveromg / Shutterstock 29

Printed in the United States of America.

HC 10 9 8 7 6 5 4 3 2 1
PB 10 9 8 7 6 5 4 3 2 1

Table of Contents

Let's Go Camping! 4

Camping Gear 8

Safety First 16

Where to Go 24

Have Fun! 28

Glossary 30

Read More 31

Websites 31

Index 32

Let's Go Camping!

You are sitting around a crackling fire. Your family and friends are with you. They laugh and smile. Everyone talks about the day's adventures. Some of them hiked through the woods. Others went swimming and canoeing. What led to all this fun? Camping! Camping is a great way to spend time outdoors.

It is fun to spend time outdoors
with family on a camping trip!

This family camps in an **RV**. It's like taking a house to the campground.

 What is the most common type of camping?

Have you been camping before? If not, don't worry. There is a type of camping for everyone. Some people drive up to their campsites in RVs. They bring all the comforts of home with them. RVs have running water and kitchens. Other people hike to their campsites. They sleep in tents. They cook over open fires.

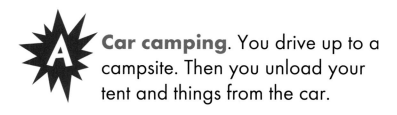

Car camping. You drive up to a campsite. Then you unload your tent and things from the car.

Camping Gear

Where will you sleep? That's the first thing to think about. An RV or camper has beds inside. Many campers sleep in an RV. Most do not, though. About 80 percent of campers sleep in tents. They curl up in a sleeping bag at night. The ground can be hard to sleep on. Tent campers often bring an air mattress or sleeping pad.

Even though tents are just poles and fabric, they can help keep campers warm and dry.

Campers can use a gas cook stove to make hot meals outside.

 Is it safe to drink water from rivers and lakes?

Campers have to eat. They use roasting sticks to cook hotdogs over a fire. **S'mores** are an easy treat to make over the fire. But for other meals, campers have a whole camp kitchen. They have a cook stove and bring things like pots, dishes, and silverware. But remember, you can't store food in the fridge. You will need a cooler with ice.

 No! The water is unclean and can make you sick. Campers bring drinking water to their campsite.

Many people camp in the summer when the weather is nice. But campers are ready for all kinds of weather. A hat is good for sunny days. A rain poncho is handy in case it rains. A hot day can turn into a cold night. Prepared campers bring along something warm to wear, like a sweatshirt and long pants.

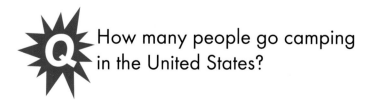

How many people go camping in the United States?

A poncho keeps this camper dry on a rainy day. The weather is not always sunny!

About 40 million!

Swimming is a fun outdoor activity to do while camping.

 Can I bring my pets camping?

Now think about fun things to do. Outdoor fun is what camping is all about. The most popular thing to do is hiking. Some campers even go biking. Many campers find a pool or lake for swimming. They might even find a fishing hole. Some campers bring **binoculars** for bird watching.

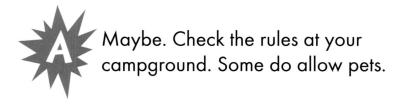 Maybe. Check the rules at your campground. Some do allow pets.

Safety First

Camping is fun. But campers need to stay safe. Safe campers never go anywhere alone. And they always tell someone where they are going. The outdoors can be a big place to get lost.

Safe campers also obey the campground's safety rules. The rules may warn about **poison ivy**, damaged trails, or dangerous animals.

 What if I get lost?

This sign warns campers that bears are around. The rules help keep people safe.

BEAR COUNTRY

Store all food in vehicle
Read bulletin board regulations
All wildlife are dangerous.

REGISTER
BEFORE
ENTERING
CAMPGROUND

It's a good idea to carry a whistle. Stay where you are, and blow the whistle 3 times in a row so people can find you.

The woods are filled with animals. There are birds and raccoons, and sometimes even bears! They usually won't bother you. But the smell of food can attract them to a campsite. Car campers keep food in their car at night. **Wilderness campers** hang food from a tree away from the tent.

 What should we do with our trash?

These bears got into a camper's cooler! Keep food where animals can't find it.

 Trash from food should go into a covered trash can away from the campsite. Raccoons and bears might try to dig through it for a treat.

Fire is dangerous. Safe campers make sure the fire is out before they leave the site.

 **Q** Is it okay to cut down trees for firewood?

Campfires can be a very fun part of camping. But they can also be very dangerous. Fires should not be left unattended. A spark could fly onto the tent or land on the ground. That could lead to a forest fire. Even just coals can cause trouble. Campers pour water on them until they are no longer red-hot.

 No! Campgrounds have rules against this. You will need to buy firewood.

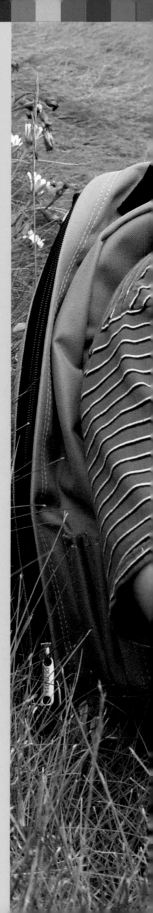

Being outside means exposure to bugs and sun. Campers pack bug spray to stop bug bites. They pack sunblock to protect from sunburn.

Even careful campers can get hurt. It is wise to have a basic **first aid kit**. Bandages and ointments for bites and stings can be handy.

A basic first aid kit has items that help treat minor cuts and bites.

22

Where to Go

If you have never been camping, you can set up a tent in your backyard. That's a safe and easy way to start camping. After a couple nights, you will get used to sleeping outdoors.

Do you want to camp in comfort? Try a **resort** or large campground. They have electric and water hook-ups for RVs. Most also have swimming pools.

Set up a tent in the backyard
for an easy night of camping.

Wilderness campers hike to their site. These campers need to pack light!

 Can I camp at a national park?

Are you ready to be more adventurous? Try a county or state park. They have some great campgrounds. Most sites are for car camping. But some parks also have areas for wilderness camping. Campers carry all their gear in a backpack and hike to the campsite.

 Yes! Many have campsites. The busiest US national park is Great Smoky Mountains National Park.

Have Fun!

Camping is not just about sleeping in a tent or sitting around a campfire roasting marshmallows. Camping is about spending time with family and friends. It's about enjoying the outdoors. Campers hike or explore nature. They go kayaking or rock climbing. But mostly, camping is about having fun. Enjoy!

Families enjoy the great outdoors on camping trips.

Glossary

binoculars A tool that helps people see objects that are far away.

car camping A type of camping which involves driving to your campsite with all of your gear in your car.

first aid kit A kit of supplies such as bandages and ointments that can be used for medical emergencies.

poison ivy A plant that can cause redness, itching, and blisters on the skin if touched.

resort A vacation spot that has lots of things to make your stay fun; camping resorts often have pools, arcades, and planned activities.

RV Short for recreational vehicle, RVs have living space inside; many have beds, refrigerators, bathrooms, and TVs.

s'mores A treat made of graham crackers, chocolate, and roasted marshmallows.

wilderness camping A type of camping that involves hiking to your campsite while carrying all of your gear; also called backcountry camping.

Read More

Hardyman, Robyn. *Camping*. New York: Windmill Books, 2014.

Hoena, Blake. *Campfire Crisis*. Adventure Kids. Minneapolis: Lake 7 Creative, 2013.

Snyder, Adeline. *Camping*. New York: Gareth Stevens Pub., 2013.

Time for Kids. *The Book of How: All About Survival*. New York: Time Home Entertainment Inc., 2011.

Websites

Boy Scout Trail: Camping Recipes
www.boyscouttrail.com/boy-scouts/boy-scout-recipes.asp

Kids Camping
www.kidscamping.com

Smokey Kids
www.smokeybear.com/kids/

Index

animals 16, 18
biking 15
bug spray 22
campfire 4, 11, 21, 28
car camping 7, 18, 27
cooking 7, 11
first aid kit 22
fishing 15
food 11, 18
hiking 4, 7, 27, 28
national parks 26, 27
pets 14, 15

resorts 24
RVs 7, 8, 24
safety 16
sleeping 8, 24
state parks 27
sunblock 22
swimming 4, 15
tents 7, 8, 24, 28
water 10, 11
weather 12
wilderness camping 18, 27

About the Author

Some of Allan Morey's favorite memories from his childhood were spend with his grandparents. While hiking, fishing, and camping with them, he grew to enjoy the outdoors. He still does those things, only now he takes his wife and kids with him. They enjoy having campfires and making s'mores as much as he does.